GW01269816

CASTLES OF THE WEST COUNTRY
COLOURING AND ACTIVITY BOOK

D. C. Perkins, B.A. (Hons.), M.Ed., Ph.D. (Wales).

Illustrations by Craig Hildrew

© D C and E J Perkins, 1993.

No reproduction of this book in whole or in part is allowed except with the written permission of the publishers.

DOMINO BOOKS (WALES) LTD.,
P O Box 32,
Swansea SA1 1FN.

Typeset by Domino Books (Wales) Ltd
Printed in Hong Kong

ISBN 1 85772 050 4

COLOURING AND ACTIVITY BOOKS

Castles of the West Country
My Holiday in the West Country
Mines

Trains of the West Country
The Celts
Mills

ACTIVITY PACKS

Packs can be customised for educational establishments, historic houses and tourist venues.

Castles of the West Country
Farmlife in the West Country
Forests and Reservoirs in the West
Country
Green - Conservation in the West
Country
Historic Houses in the West
Country
Mills in the West Country
Mines and Caves in the West
Country
My Holiday in the West Country
Sealife in the West Country
Trains of the West Country
Wildlife in the West Country

EARLY HISTORY PACKS
Pre-History
The Stone Age
The Bronze Age
The Iron Age
The Celts
The Romans
The Normans

THIS COLOURING AND ACTIVITY BOOK BELONGS TO

NAME _____

ADDRESS _____

_____

_____

AGE _____

ALL ABOUT CASTLES

Even the earliest men had to defend themselves from wild animals or opposing families and tribes. The history of castles and forts in the West Country goes back to 3,000 BC when in the Stone Age fortified camps were built on hills for men and cattle. They were constructed with bone or stone tools. In the Bronze Age (about 2,000 BC) more hilltop forts were built and in the Iron Age (900 - 100 BC) these forts were rebuilt or extended. These were anti-invasion strongholds and over 2,000 existed throughout the United Kingdom.

During Roman times, the whole of Britain, including the West Country, was occupied. The Romans were famous for roads and baths but they also had garrisons of soldiers billetted in forts. An example of this is Bath in Somerset.. The Roman fort established here later became a prosperous spa, Aquae Sulis.

From the 4th. to the 10th. centuries, the West Country, like the rest of Britain, was in a state of turmoil. Saxons, Angles and Danes invaded in turn and to protect themselves, people built earthworks especially around large villages and towns.

The great warrior king, William Conqueror, siezed England at the Battle of Hastings in 1066. He knew the value of castles.

A castle was a home - but it was also well protected - a fortress where people and animals were safe from attack. Castles were now built to defend vital places such as a town, a river crossing, a port, important cross roads, a border or simply to defend places already won in battle.

After the Norman Conquest, William permitted castles to be built wherever they were needed to protect a strategic interest and to maintain his control over the natives.

MOTTE AND BAILEY CASTLES

The early Norman strongholds were very simple and are known as motte and bailey castles. They consisted of a motte - a natural or artificial mound of earth - on which a wooden tower or keep was built. Most mottes were 10 - 12 metres high and were surrounded by a ditch or moat.

The motte was connected to a large outer enclosure or courtyard called a bailey. This was protected by its own ditch, moat or bank and was surrounded by a timber fence of stakes or palisade. Domestic buildings were usually placed in the bailey (e.g. the kitchens) because of the risk of fire.

Castles of this type could be constructed in a matter of weeks and when attacked, the garrison could retreat to the motte and hold out until relief arrived. All mottes had one special feature, there was no door on the ground floor. Access into the castle was always gained via an opening at first floor level and entry was by a ladder or a light footbridge which could be withdrawn to prevent a surprise attack.

STONE SHELL KEEPS

Motte and bailey castles were fairly easy to capture or set alight because they were made of wood and quickly fired. Stone came to be used instead of wood and shell keep castles emerged. These were a natural development of the earlier strongholds, a stone wall replacing the wooden stakes or palisade on top of the motte. Buildings were then erected inside the shell and these included a hall, a solar (or study), a chapel and a kitchen.

Square stone keeps were eventually built bigger and stronger. They were often up to 35 metres high, and were erected in three or four storeys with spiral staircases in the corner turrets. As the size and weight of these keeps grew, they were built on natural hills or more often on flat ground.

A typical stone keep had a basement with three storeys. The basement was for stores and prisoners, soldiers were garrisoned on the first floor, the Great Hall and the Lord's solar were on the second floor, and sleeping rooms were on the third. Roof and battlements were above. The windows were thin slits in the brickwork, just wide enough to let chinks of light in and ideal for firing arrows through at anyone daring to attack the stronghold.

Some strongholds were rectangular stone towers and these dominated the castle scene until the end of the 11th. century. To defend themselves against intruders, a series of additions were made to these stone castles. These adaptations included:

1. A forebuilding to protect the castle entrance.
2. A plinth (a rectangular slab or block of stone) to stop battering rams reaching the bottom of the walls.
3. A strong wall called a curtain wall built around the keep.
4. A gatehouse built in the curtain wall.
5. A portcullis, a thick metal grille, which could be lowered to protect the doorway into the castle.
6. The division of the castle into two sections, the inner bailey and the outer bailey. The keep stood in the

Colour this picture of a motte and bailey castle.

inner bailey, a courtyard where the kitchen, granary and other storerooms were found. Beyond was the outer bailey, a large enclosure containing domestic buildings, stables, gardens and a training and exercise area.

7. Circular keep. Rectangular keeps with their corners meant that the enemy could not always be seen. Towers were built circular or multiangular so as to give no screen to the enemy at any point.

8. Further protection of the outer bailey by high walls, D-shaped and round towers, a gatehouse, draw-bridge and moat.

DEVELOPMENT OF THE STONE KEEP

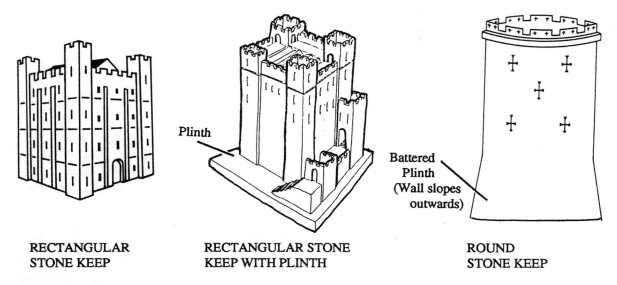

RECTANGULAR STONE KEEP

RECTANGULAR STONE KEEP WITH PLINTH

ROUND STONE KEEP

Plinth

Battered Plinth (Wall slopes outwards)

CONCENTRIC CASTLES

In the 13th. century (about 1250) a new type of castle began to be built. This was called a concentric castle. Most of those built by Edward 1st. in Wales were of this type. It had two sets of curtain walls and if intruders broke through the outer curtain, they still had to capture the inner one and were also trapped between the two and were vulnerable to attack.

A concentric castle seldom had a central keep. Instead, it had a large inner bailey and people lived in dwellings built against the walls. The outer wall was protected by a large, defensive building called a barbican and beyond that was another set of towers with a drawbridge and portcullis, the inner gatehouse.

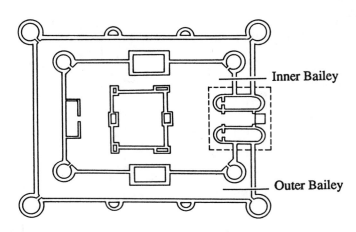

Inner Bailey

Outer Bailey

PLAN OF A CONCENTRIC CASTLE

CASTLE DEFENCES

The castle was essentially a home designed to ensure security from attack. When you visit a castle, look for the following, all of which are part of its defences.

Colour this picture of a twelfth century castle.
How does this castle differ from the castle on page 5?

The Curtain Wall

The castle's main defence. Some of the stone used in West Country castles was imported from Caen in Normandy. The thickness of the wall varied from castle to castle, the average being from 2 to 3 metres (6 to 7 feet). Caernarfon, in North Wales, has a 5 metre (15 feet) thick curtain wall. Soldiers defended the tops of the wall

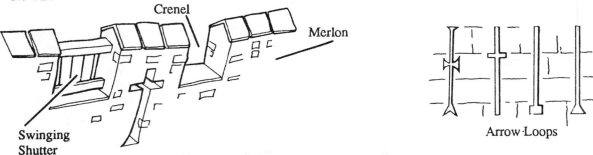

DEFENSIVE STRUCTURE OF THE CURTAIN WALL

and there were gaps in the battlements called crenels so that they could observe the enemy and fire at them. To avoid injury, the defenders shielded themselves behind merlons and swinging wooden (later iron) shutters could be closed across the crenels to give additional protection. As well as firing through the crenels and over the battlements, there were grooves in the walls big enough to fire through. These were called arrow slits or loops.

The Gatehouse

This was the main entrance to the castle and the most likely point of attack. It was very well defended and usually had a portcullis. The portcullis was a strong grating made of oak, plated and shod with iron which could be moved up and down in stone groves, clearing or blocking entry. From the portcullis a narrow passageway led inside the castle. This passage had holes in the ceiling above which could be used for dropping stones, firebrands, hot liquids and similar missiles on intruders. These holes were called machiolations. There were often openings in the walls. Called murder holes (meurtrière), pikes could be thrust through them to kill attackers.

Moat and Drawbridge

The moat was a wide water-filled ditch surrounding the castle. It was crossed by a drawbridge which could be raised to prevent access to the castle or lowered to allow people and supplies inside.

The Barbican

To protect the gatehouse, a walled outwork was often built in front of it. This was called the barbican. It was an enclosure with two towers and a whole system of defences. Often there was a dual defence system, the barbican and gatehouse having the same arrangements. Thus, there was usually a drawbridge, a portcullis, machiolations and murder holes with armed men in key positions.

Hoardings

These were added to a castle to improve its defences before attack. First, they consisted of temporary wooden structures built at the top of the walls of the castle. Later, such hoardings were made of masonry covered with slates and were permanent. Arrow holes were incorporated into the structures and there were holes in the floor through which stones, boiling liquid and other materials could be thrown on to the enemy below.

LATER CASTLES

By the end of the 15th. century, siege warfare involving castles declined. Gunpowder had been invented and walls could be more easily breached. Differences of opinion began to be settled on the open battlefield. The Welshman, Henry VII, for example, defeated Richard III at Bosworth Field (1485).

Wealthy people began to live in manor houses. But there was still a need for castles. Henry VII and VIII annoyed the French from time to time and there was every possibility of invasion from across the Channel. Thus, coastal castles were built against invasion and many of the old castles repaired. Henry VIII in particular built a series of artillery forts (for example, at St. Mawes and Pendennis in Cornwall and Portland in Dorset)

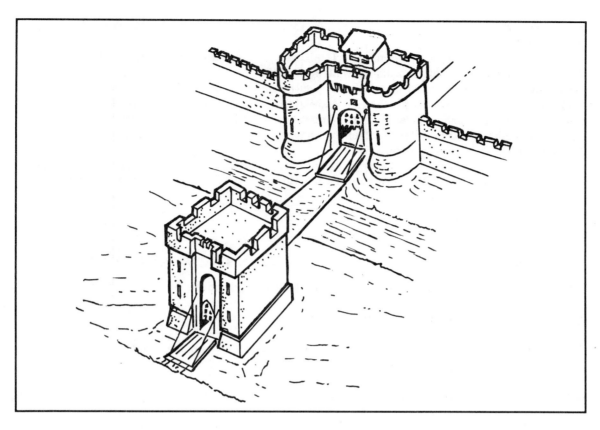

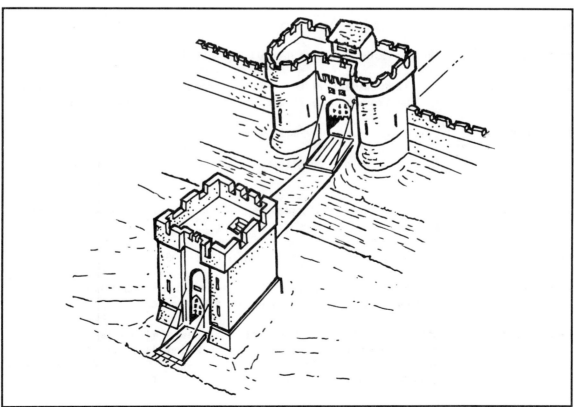

These are two pictures of a barbican and gatehouse. Find ten differences between the two pictures.

to offer resistance to the enemy. They carried on the idea of the concentric castle but increased the number of deflecting surfaces.

It is sometimes thought that by the end of the 15th. century, traditional castles had outlived their usefulness. But this is untrue. The strength of mediaeval walls against gunfire was proved in the English Civil War (1642 - 1651) for many old castles could not be captured even by crack troops with the latest 17th. century artillery. Again, when Napoleon threatened in the 18th. and early 19th. centuries, coastal defences including ancient castles were reinforced to rebuff him. New structures called Martello towers were erected. When Adolf Hitler presented a similar threat in 1940 and another programme of up-dating defences was begun, the British army used many of Henry VIII's castles effectively.

In the 19th. and 20th centuries, castles were of three types. Some buildings called castles were in reality fortified manor houses, some mediaeval castles were made more comfortable to live in, e.g. Compton Castle in Devonshire.

CASTLE DEVELOPMENT IN THE WEST COUNTRY

3,000 BC	Rough Stone Age structures built with primitive tools.
2,000 BC	Bronze Age. Forts on hills.
900 - 100 BC	Iron Age. Forts often developed from earlier buildings. Mainly designed to protect tribes against surprise attack.
AD 43	Roman forts built after invasion and occupation.
500 - 1,000	Angles, Saxons and Danes invade. Towns fortified against attack.
1066	Norman Conquest. Many motte and bailey castles speedily built.
11th. century	Wooden castles, but some already being built of stone.
12. - 13th. centuries	More stone castles built. Development of stone keeps. Many ideas brought back from the Crusades in the Middle East incorporated into the new castles.
14th. century	Concentric castles and walled towns.
15th. century	Return to more basic, simple castle structures: comfort the keynote. Manor houses developed.
16th. century	Tudors built shore forts for protection especially against the French e.g. St. Mawes, Pendennis and Portland.
17th. century	Mediaeval castles used in the Civil War 1642 - 1651.
18th. century	Country mansions developed. Called 'castles' often for reasons of prestige or grandeur but were really large houses with fortifications.
19th. century	Many shore forts - Martello towers built - in case of a Napoleonic invasion. Reinforcement of shore defences. Some castles built by the wealthy (fortified manor houses) or added to for prestige, e.g. Sudeley Castle and Castle Drogo (actually built between 1910 and 1930 by Sir Edwin Hutyens)
20th. century	Shore forts reinforced for defence against Germany (1914 - 18 and 1939 - 45 World Wars). Pill boxes also built and some of these still remain.

THINGS TO DO

1. **Draw a plan of a castle you have visited.**

2. **The following may be found in a castle. What are they?**

   TTEOM, EPKE, LAIYBE, TRAUCNI LWLA, OGTEUESAH,
   INBRBAAC, DRMEUR LSOEH, URLPCLISOT,
   OLPO, TOMA.

3. **The following may be found in a castle.**

   1 and 4 Pulled up in case of attack.
   2 Temporary wooden structure at the top
      of a castle wall.
   3 and 9 Found at the top of a battlement.
   5 and 7 Used to break down doors and walls.
   6 Fired arrows.
   8 Lord's private room.
   10 Where important functions were held.

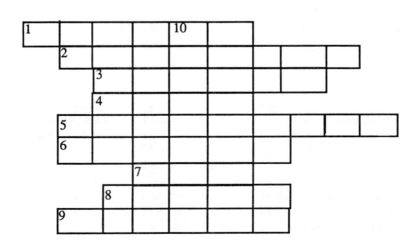

LIVING IN A CASTLE

In the Middle Ages a lord or baron moved around the country a great deal. The household rarely settled anywhere for any length of time but in winter often stayed within the castle walls.

Inside, a castle was a community which was carefully organised like a small town or village. The inhabitants belonged to the military or to the domestic life of the castle.

Military

The most important people were the baron and his wife, and their family. Under the baron's command were his knights. These may have been as few as a dozen or as many as fifty. The knights were served by pages and squires, boys and young men usually of noble birth, being trained to become knights. The armourer was also important. He looked after the stocks of weapons and armour: such things as bows, bow-strings, bolts, arrows, helmets and swords. He repaired armour and kept this and weapons free from rust by cleaning them with sand and vinegar. He also sharpened swords and was often responsible for maintaining larger defensive weapons like catapults.

Domestic

The most important person in the castle after the baron was his steward. He acted as his deputy and dealt with legal matters, appointed officials such as bailiffs and reeves, fixed tenancies and rents and supervised the smooth running of the castle. He was the treasurer in charge of all accounts and he was responsible for the castle when the baron was away. Below the steward was a whole host of minor officials: a chaplain, huntsmen, falconers, grooms, cooks, domestic servants, smiths, masons and carpenters.

Preparing meals for those in the castle was a major task. Sheep and pigs were kept for meat; chickens, swans and geese were reared for meat and eggs while cows and goats provided milk. Oats, barley and wheat, apples, plums and pears were grown outside the castle.

A castle was a very busy place with most people working from dawn until dusk: fetching water, wood for fuel, grooming horses, washing and mending clothes, brewing ale, baking bread: all the daily chores necessary in a self sufficient community. A priest said morning prayers and taught the pages. Every boy learned how to use weapons and there was regular weapon training. The lady of the castle or an apothecary helped to make ointments and care for the sick.

Cooking

In early castles food was prepared in a wooden shed in a courtyard. Later castles had kitchens. Much of the meat (venison, boars, hares and rabbits) was roasted on fixed metal rods called spits above the kitchen fire or open hearth. A servant boy was employed to turn these spits so that the meat roasted evenly. There was no butter and fat dripping from the meat was precious and as much as possible was caught in bowls. Large bronze cooking pots called cauldrons were used to cook soups while bread was baked in an oven at the back or near the open hearth. Spices and herbs were used widely. Without refrigeration, food, especially meat, often went bad. In the summer, the household lived well and many courses would be carried to the Great Hall by servants and served by squires. The dishes included chicken and squirrel broth, salmon with orange, trout with spices, shellfish scented with herbs, sugared mackerel, roasted swan, roasted venison, boar's head with brawn, roast beef with chopped herbs, blancmange (a savoury dish in these times), stuffed quarter of bear, fresh fruit tarts, fig pudding, apple dumplings, cakes with honey and roasted chestnuts or nuts. Sometimes, especially in winter, food was scarce and even the wealthy were forced to live on meagre rations such as beans and gruel (a thin porridge).

Eating

The most important meals were eaten in the Great Hall, the centre of life in a castle. Only the baron, his wife and special guests had chairs. These were arranged around a raised table, the high table. The other tables were just boards on trestles. Everyone who lived in the castle ate together. Feast nights began at 5 pm and lasted for hours with often six to eight meat courses and over twenty dishes for each course. Squires served the 'top table' and pages served the lower tables. The baron and his family and his special guests may have eaten from pewter plates and had knives and spoons (there were no forks) but most people ate with their fingers, throwing scraps and bones on to the floor where dogs devoured them. Generally, food was served on huge slabs of bread called trenchers. Top table drank wine out of pewter goblets, whilst the servants, journeymen and apprentices drank beer from clay mugs. Food from one trencher was usually shared by two people and people also shared goblets and mugs.

Colour this picture of a banquet in the Great Hall of a Castle.

Washing

Water was very precious in the Middle Ages and often had to be carried from wells or rivers by servants. People, especially the lower classes, were not able to wash often. Soap was rare and people merely splashed themselves with water. The baron and his family used soap made of mutton fat, wood ash and soda. Men imagined that bathing reduced their strength and bathed rarely. The bath was a large wooden chest or barrel and bathing was something of an event. Water had to be heated and carried by the servants. The soap was soft and evil smelling so herbs and flowers were sprinkled on the water. The baron's wife bathed in the water first and then the other women took their turn. People did not clean their teeth and most suffered in later life from toothache and tooth decay. Until 1400, surgeon barbers believed in extracting only loose teeth and relied on crude instruments for carrying out such operations.

Garderobes (toilets) were usually holes in the wall with long chutes. They were unhealthy, stinking and unpleasant. There were only a few garderobes in a mediaeval castle and they were often shared by a whole garrison although the baron and his family may have had their own. There were no disinfectants.

Sleeping

The baron and his family and special guests were the only people who slept off the floor on wooden frame beds filled with straw. A mattress was on top of this and the bed was surrounded by curtains giving some privacy and protection from draughts and the cold. Most people slept on pallets on the floor, mattresses stuffed with straw and feathers which could be rolled up out of the way in the day. Nobody had a bedroom to himself. Several of the baron's servants slept in the same room as well as his children and dogs. Most of the household slept in their day clothes in the kitchen or Great Hall. Here it was warm and when they woke, they were dressed and ready for work.

THINGS TO DO

WORDSQUARE

Find the following in the word square:
(Each letter may be used more than once or not at all.)

1. Pulled up in case of attack.

2. Safest part of a castle.

3. Poet.

4. Head of a castle.

5. Castles.

6. Defensive wall.

7. Shot from a bow.

8. Coat -- ----.

9. Surrounds a castle and is full of water.

10. Aperture for arrows.

11. Battle between knights.

B	R	I	D	G	E	K	Y
A	Y	L	O	R	D	E	C
R	O	O	F	O	C	E	U
D	U	O	F	O	F	P	R
W	D	P	I	M	O	A	T
A	R	R	O	W	R	A	A
L	A	R	M	S	T	D	I
L	W	J	O	U	S	T	N

Colour this picture of a knight.

KNIGHTS AND ARMOUR

A knight in armour conjures up a romantic picture of life in the Middle Ages. It seems as if there was always something to fight about from land to the honour of a maiden. Much of the fighting in castles was done man to man and armour was developed to protect men from their foes. A knight was an armoured horse-soldier known as a 'man-at-arms'. Armour changed constantly throughout mediaeval times. The earliest suits were a coat of mail with a shield and iron helmet. These were gradually replaced by pieces of 'plate armour', a protective covering iron shell, until by the 15th. century, the knight was completely encased in iron. The mail protected the most vulnerable parts of the body. The weight of these suits became a problem. A knight sometimes became very hot and tired, and some died of heat stroke during a long battle. Armour became so cumbersome that when a knight fell down, it was difficult for him to get up. Encased in armour, all knights looked the same. Because of this a method of picture writing developed. These were special designs on a shield or armour which identified a knight or his lord. Such pictures were the personal heraldic coats of arms of a leader.

COATS OF ARMS
The earliest known coat of arms was that of Geoffrey of Anjou who when knighted by his father in law, Henry I of England, received a shield decorated with lions from the King. Many shields incorporated lions, crowns, castles, animals and keys on the front: symbols of strength, bravery, power or possession.

TOURNAMENTS AND JOUSTS
From time to time, tournaments and jousts were held to improve military training, as entertainment, or to celebrate an engagement, marriage or birth. The baron, his wife and important guests watched from specially built arenas or tents. The area where battle took place was called the lists. The events consisted of tourneys in which two armies fought each other or jousts when two knights on horseback charged at each other with long lances and tried to knock each other to the ground. In between them was a wooden barrier called a tilt which stopped the horses crashing into each other. It was usual for lances to be shattered in such jousts. If the lances of both knights were broken, they often dismounted to continue their duel with swords. To prepare for a tournament or joust, young squires often practised riding at a 'quintain', a target with a weight attached which would swing and hit a rider who did not move out of the way quickly enough.

OTHER PASTIMES, GAMES AND AMUSEMENTS
Favourite sports of these times included hunting for hares, rabbits and boars with deer being the preserve of the King or nobility. In falconry, peregrines, eagles and goshawks were trained to attack and bring back prey such as hares or rabbits or other birds.

'Bandy ball' was a very rough type of hockey in which a player was allowed to hit his opponent with a stick. There was also a form of tennis in which the ball was hit by the palm of the hand instead of a racquet. In winter, skating on ice with iron skates was popular. Indoors, chess was a favourite and dice were much used in gambling. Few people owned books because they had to be written by hand and few could read, but story telling was a much enjoyed pastime, especially swapping jokes together with singing and dancing. In large castles, there might be entertainment by a harpist or minstrels and sometimes jugglers and acrobats were hired to entertain special guests.

Colour this picture of a joust.

ATTACK!

It is early summer in the year of Our Lord 1399. Baron Gilbert, a powerful Lord and landowner in Devonshire seeks more land. He has many serfs to produce crops for him and many animals which need new grazing: they must be fed now so that they can be slaughtered and salted to provide food for the long winter months.

The Baron decides to attack Lord Montfort, a neighbour whom he dislikes and who has caused the Baron a great deal of trouble in the past.

He has to gain entry through the thick walls of the castle and also overcome the defence that will be mounted from within by Montfort's men. If the castle cannot be taken quickly, then he must prepare to lay siege to it. Baron Gilbert lays his plans carefully.

1. He must attack when the castle is most vulnerable, unexpectedly at night when there is no moon or early in the morning, preferably at dawn.

2. He must place spies within the castle to report on the state of its defences: the number of men, their weapons and equipment, the disposition of troops and the stocks of food supplies. Is the well full of drinking water and can it be contaminated with salt?

3. The Baron must ensure that relief supplies, especially food and water, cannot reach the castle if it cannot be taken quickly. Also no one must be able to leave the castle and seek help from one of Montfort's brothers.

4. The Baron has to decide how to arm his soldiers and where to place them. He has to prepare to lay siege to the castle.

The following is based on his notebooks.

Sapping
After advancing along an open trench, then under camouflage, the sappers loosened several stones of the outer wall of the castle. They then dug out the rubble inside. Once entry was achieved, the wall was shored up with props. Faggots covered with lard were piled in the hole in the wall and set alight. This method of attack known as mining with firebrands would cause the wall to collapse at that point. (The debris usually fell into the moat making a bridge for the attackers to cross.)

Mining
More complicated than sapping which took place above ground. Mining involved digging a mine deep underground, digging under the moat and than attacking the base of a castle wall or tower. Once the wall was reached, it could be breached by sapping.

Siege Weapons
He might use a belfry or seige tower (or several of them). A siege tower was placed against the wall of a castle. It consisted of a ladder and an attacking platform. At its base was a compartment which sheltered the attackers during the approach to the castle. The attackers scaled ladders to reach the platform. The belfry also had devices for throwing missiles such as stones and dead carcasses over the castle wall.

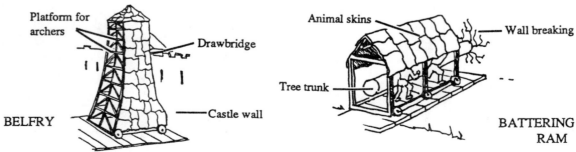

Platform for archers — Drawbridge — Castle wall — BELFRY

Animal skins — Wall breaking — Tree trunk — BATTERING RAM

Battering Ram
This was an iron-tipped tree trunk carried within a protective covering, a wagon-like structure on wheels. It

Colour this picture of a castle under attack.

was operated by 10 or 12 men, depending on its size and was slung from ropes. They reached the gate or wall and swung the ram backwards and forwards so as to set up a formidable pendulum-like movement which had considerable destructive power.

Basic Rock Drills
These were also used against castle walls. Two drills were popular, one using levers and the other driven by a bow. They drilled holes in the walls leading to its collapse.

The Trebucket
This was a type of catapult with a large weight in front. The enormous sling was used to hurl boulders and huge rocks over the castle wall.

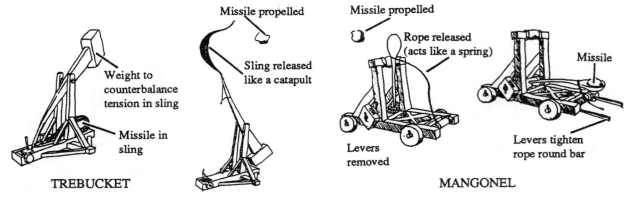

TREBUCKET   MANGONEL

The Mangonel
This was another type of catapult. It was also used to throw large quantities of small stones, burning brands and dead carcasses over the walls.

The Scorpion
This catapult was less powerful than the trebucket or mangonel. It was useful because it could be assembled on the spot.

The Ballista
The ballista or perrier was a smaller weapon. Again like a catapult, it was used for firing fist-sized stones at the enemy. It was usually used against men and archers rather than against gatehouses or castle walls.

Light Catapults
There were a number of light catapults used, all designed to attack the castle outside and within.

The Great Pivoting Crossbow
This was mounted on a three-wheeled carriage and could fire a boar-spear 5 metres long (known as a 'garrot') over a distance of 50 metres. It was most effective against infantry and cavalry sent out to combat an army besieging a castle.

Other Aids to Attack
Ladders known as **escalades** were used to scale the walls. Having scaled the walls, the attackers used **small artillery** to hurl rocks, stones and burning material at those within the castle. Ladders with movable parts with extending sections (like a fireman's ladder) were also used. A **siege engine,** known as a cat or stork and sometimes mounted on wheels was used by archers.

There were a number of devices to protect attacking forces. These included **mantlets,** transportable screens from which archers and cross bowmen could fire at the enemy and not be hit themselves. Individuals also protected themselves by covering themselves with a wicker, a **wicker siege basket.** Sappers who were responsible for weakening and destroying the walls also had a number of protective devices. For example, the **sapper's cat** or vine was protected by wood covered by hides, turf or even dung. This was winched along. The **sapper's 'mouse'** was used in the same way as a mantlet to enable attackers to get near the wall they intended to sap. It was then turned round so that sappers could work in the safety of its cover.

THINGS TO DO

1. The following are used to attack a castle. What are they?

   RWORAS, ACPTTUAL, EEGIS GNNEEI, LEYFRB, RAEGTBNIT MRA, PPSIAGN

   LTEMATN, BHCTTREEU, DDLARE, LLSITAAB.

2. Which two shields are the same?

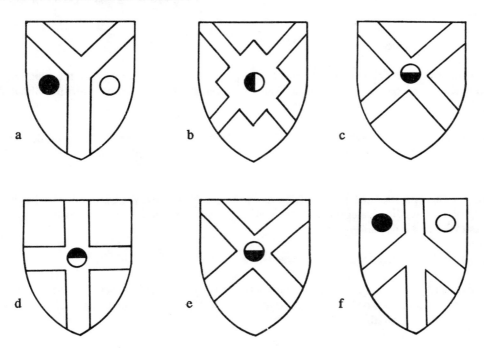

3. My first is in king but not in queen.
   My second is in night but not in day.
   My third is in ink but not in pen.
   My fourth is in good but not in bad.
   My fifth is in hand but not in band.
   My last is in two and also in three.
   My whole lives in a castle.

   What am I?

4. Find ten words in SIEGE ENGINE.

DEFENCE

A castle is a fortress with many devices to defend itself against attack and protect its inhabitants. The moat is deep and not easily crossed. The drawbridge when raised makes entry to the castle very difficult. The barbican and gatehouse are strong and well defended with machiolations, holes in the ceiling, through which the invaders can be attacked and holes in the walls through which sharp pikes could be thrust. The castle walls are not easily broken or scaled and provided cover for those inside the castle. Arrow slits for cross bows and for long bows, catapults for throwing projectiles at attackers, hoardings for throwing material down on attackers such as boiling water and boiling oil provided a very effective defensive system. If an attempt is made to tunnel under the defences and emerge within the castle walls, a counter mine may be dug. This is a mine dug above that of the invader allowing the lower mine to be flooded. The most formidable weapon for an attacker is often to lay siege to the castle, to wait until time wastes the resources and the will of those imprisoned in the castle.

The following is based on extracts from Lady Ann's diary.

It is the silence, the strange quiet, which is the most disturbing. We were all asleep when the attack first came. The noise sent us scurrying about in panic. Then there was the smell of burning and the whine of arrows.

Someone had lowered the drawbridge and jammed it so that it could not easily be lifted. My brother died raising it. Fortunately, the moat was deep and once the drawbridge was raised, my father was able to organise everyone.

The small fires the enemy started within the castle walls were quickly doused.We burned their belfry and poured burning oil and scalding water on to the men using the battering ram. A few marauders had even managed to scale the castle walls.

By daybreak the attackers were driven back. It was slight relief.

My father seethed with rage. Only a few weeks earlier Baron Gilbert had stayed here, had accepted my father's hospitality. Undoubtedly he had taken the opportunity to spy out the castle and probably knew as much about our defences as we did. Treachery. A betrayal of friendship.

It was soon apparent that our walls could not be breached and the castle would not be taken easily. We had a good store of supplies and the water in the well was fresh and no one had tampered with it.

But we had not reckoned with the determination of Baron Gilbert. He and his men camped around the castle and the siege began again.

For weeks we have been surrounded. A messenger sent out under cover of darkness to seek help from my uncle was captured and his dead, mutilated body hurled over the walls. Once we heard the attackers digging under the castle but we were able to flood their mine. At night we can see the lights of our tormentors encamped below the walls, hear their voices, and their loud singing. Their bawdry songs mock and make fun of us, promising that no one shall survive.

When the battle was as its height, I fetched and carried for the men at arms. During the siege I have spent much of the time looking after the injured. My mother overcome by the death of my brother has been able to do little. Those laying siege to us show little interest in the battle. True anyone unwise enough to put his head over the castle walls is likely to be shot at but it seems that Gilbert's final plan is to starve us into submission. And he may succeed. The stores are now depleted and the water in the well is low. Now that the injured have either recovered or died there is little to do but wait and wonder what will become of us. I pray to God we shall survive.

Colour this picture of the defence of a castle.

PRISONS AND TORTURE

Few early castles had special prisons. Prisoners were held below the keep or where goods were stored. Later, prisons were designed as such but they were mainly for hostages held for ransom and therefore well treated.

Conditions for ordinary prisoners were brutal. Thrown into a damp, dark room, left without food or water, often manacled by their hands and feet, they lay helpless until they starved to death.In the early Middle Ages there was little torture but there was trial by battle or ordeal. Torture developed when the Church tried to extract confessions from heretics.

The methods spread outside the Church and included putting a prisoner under a board and adding weights on top of it until he confessed to his 'crimes', using red hot pokers to burn a man's skin or remove his eyes. Branding prisoners with a specially designed branding iron also became fashionable. Some prisoners had to endure iron collars and others were fitted with iron masks. The scold's bridle was intended to be used mainly on women. Placed over the victim's head like a cage, it had a piece of metal which fitted into the woman's mouth to stop her from talking. Thumbscrews squashed the thumbs and fingers and later there was the rack: this was designed to stretch the body slowly, a little more each day so that the body was filled with pain.

HAUNTED CASTLES

Many people were mistreated or starved to death in castles and it is little wonder that there are many stories of such places being haunted. Few ghosts have been seen but many claim that strange noises can be heard in castles: knocking, the clanking of chains, phantom music or the howl of a dog. One of the ghosts in Berry Pomeroy Castle is said to be Margaret de Pomeroy starved to death by her sister: they both fell in love with the same man.

THINGS TO DO

A message smuggled out of the besieged castle read

DV ZIV YVHRVTVW.   KOVZHV HVMW SVOK.

What did it mean?

Code used

A	B	C	D	E	F	G	H	I	J	K	L	M
Z	Y	X	W	V	U	T	S	R	Q	P	O	N

N	O	P	Q	R	S	T	U	V	W	X	Y	Z
M	L	K	J	I	H	G	F	E	D	C	B	A

The reply promised help.

I WILL SEND FIFTY KNIGHTS AT ONCE.

Write the reply in code.

Colour this picture of prisoners in a castle dungeon.

THINGS TO DO AND THINGS TO LOOK FOR WHEN YOU VISIT A CASTLE

A visit to a castle is much more exciting and interesting if you know what probably happened in each part and why it was built in a particular way. Although daily life in castles was humdrum and filled with routine chores, castles were the scenes of historic events, battles, sieges, the births and deaths of nobility and the centres of mediaeval community life. Whoever held the castle ruled the land and its people locally.

Make Your Own Castle Plans
First, draw a diagram of the layout of the castle. Often there is a guide book to help with this. Once the basic plan is drawn, mark the positions of such features as the outer walls, keep, great tower, gatehouse, barbican, moat, portcullis and drawbridge.

It is likely that the castle is in ruins so look for signs that show where these structures once were. Walk through the castle and imagine the many people who once lived there.

History
Find out when and why the castle was built. Have there been other castles on the same site? Have any famous people been associated with it? Who owned the castle in the past and who owns it today? Who looks after it today? Has it been associated with any important events such as battles or sieges?

Checklist
1. Look at the location of the castle. Is it on a hill or a slope? Is it built on a river bank or on the coast? Is it located on a rock? Has it got easy access to the sea or water? (e.g., Restormel and St. Michael's Mount Castles.)

2. Consider the outside of the castle from the point of view of defence. How good would the defences have been?

3. Look for signs of a moat which may have disappeared. (Sometimes these have been filled in or grassed or used as car parks.)

4. Look for the curtain wall and note how thick it is. Look for the gaps in the battlements, the crenels and the parts of the wall, the merlons, designed to give shelter to those defending the castle. If it is safe to do so, walk on the battlements.

5. Look for the keep. If there is a keep, look for fireplaces: these indicate the number of floors. Holes in walls show where the joists for the floors were. Look for the remains of a spiral staircase in a turret. Look for rooms used as stores, bedrooms, studies or kitchen.

6. Consider the entrance to the castle. Look for the barbican and the gatehouse. Look for machiolations, holes in the ceiling enabling invaders to be attacked from above. Look for meurtrières or murder holes, holes in the walls through which pikes could be thrust.

7. Do you think there was a portcullis? Grooves in the barbican or gatehouse walls will show where this was.

8. Was there a drawbridge? If so the walls in the gatehouse will have large holes where the ropes or chains used to be.

9. Fireplaces and holes high up in the walls show where floors and rooms used to be.

10. Holes in the walls may show where there used to be beams that held up ceilings.

11. The shape of some rooms will be easy to tell from what is left.

12. In towers and turrets, you should see the remains of spiral staircases leading to rooms above.

13. Lines of stones against inside walls will show the position of buildings inside the castle.

Name these castles.

1. P - - - - - - - -

2. P - - - - - - - -

3. B - - - - P - - - - - -

4. S - M - - - - - - ' - M - - - -

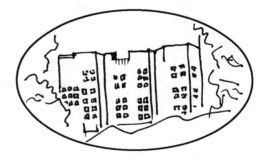

5. C - - - - - D - - - -

6. T - - - - - - -

7. S - - - - - - - -

8. D - - - - - -

14. Holes in floors might have other explanations e.g. in a courtyard, a hole may indicate a well. Adjacent to a room, a hole may have been a garderobe (a toilet).

15. The size of a room can often be guessed. The Great Hall (the main place for a banquet and gatherings) will be the biggest. The windows, or spaces where they were, will be big and there will be fireplaces against the curtain wall.

16. The place where food was prepared may be discoloured. Look for evidence of a huge fireplace big enough to roast a whole deer. Also there may be a sink, drains, or hooks and spits on which meat and pots were hung for cooking.

17. If there is a basement, look for evidence that prisoners were held there. Some castles still have rings of iron on the wall showing where prisoners were manacled.

18. Look through arrow slits and imagine how archers took aim.

19. Examine the thickness of the walls. It must have taken a lot of effort to collect the stones needed and build such walls. If possible look for debris which may have been used to fill the insides of the walls. This may give a clue to the age of the castle because this practice was discontinued in the 14th. century.

20. Consider the advantages and disadvantages of living in the castles you have visited.

21. Consider the strengths and weaknesses of the castle when it was under attack. How would you defend the castle from attack?

SOME CASTLES TO VISIT IN THE WEST COUNTRY

Avon

Thornbury

Cornwall

Launceston
Pendennis
Restormel
St. Mawes
St. Michael's Mount
Tintagel

Devonshire

Berry Pomeroy
Castle Drogo
Compton
Dartmouth
Lydford
Okehampton
Powderham
Tiverton
Totnes

Dorset

Christchurch
Corfe
Portland
Sherborne

Somerset

Dunster
Farleigh Hungerford
Nunney
Taunton

Wiltshire

Old Sarum
Old Wardour

CASTLES OF THE WEST COUNTRY

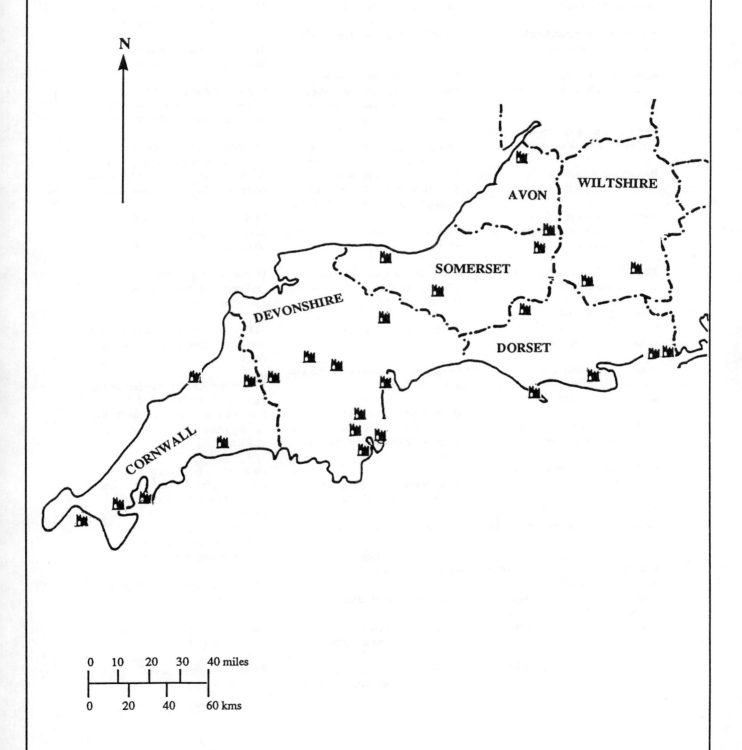

Name the castles marked on this map.

GLOSSARY

Adulterine castle: a stronghold built without royal permission.

Allure: a wall walk within the battlements of a castle.

Ashlar: square stone blocks used for facing castle walls.

Bailey: a courtyard or enclosure around a castle. Sometimes called a **ward.**

Ballista: a huge crossbow used to hurl rocks: a siege weapon.

Banquette: a raised platform to fire from placed behind a rampart.

Barbican: a tower built for defence, usually sited in front of the castle gatehouse.

Baronial Hall: the main hall of a castle or mansion.

Battering ram: an iron-tipped tree trunk used to try to knock down castle gates and walls.

Bastion: a projecting part of a castle to aid defence. Sometimes it was as large as a tower.

Battlements: the top of the walls of a castle. See merlons.

Belfry (belfrey): a siege tower used to attack a castle.

Brace: a low platform used to check attackers on lower walls of a castle.

Brattice: a wooden platform built out from the battlements which could be used to drop missiles on attackers below. Also known as **hoardings.** Later, replaced by machiolations.

Bulwarks: defensive walls of a castle.

Casemates: galleries established at the bottom of castle walls so that defenders could fire directly at miners, sappers and those using battering rams and similar besiegers.

Chemise: outer curtain wall of a castle.

Concentric castle: a castle with a system of walls each enclosing the other. The inner walls were able to fire over the outer ones.

Crenel: a space in the top of a battlement. They were divided into merlons (the stonework) and embrasures (spaces). Castles are described as having crenellated walls.

Curtain: the outer wall surrounding a bailey.

Cross-slits: a type of fissure for defending soldiers to fire through at an enemy.

Ditch: a dry or wet moat surrounding a castle.

Donjon: another name for the keep of a castle.

Drawbridge: a wooden bridge at the entrance to a castle which could be raised or lowered by chains or levers.

Embrasure: an opening at the top of a castle wall. See crenel.

Garderobe: a toilet or latrine.

Gatehouse: strongly defended entrance to a castle.

Hoarding: see **brattice.**

Keep: the main central tower of a castle. Also called a **donjon.**

Machiolation: a stone structure built out from the battlements which

had holes in its floor. These holes were used to drop missiles on attackers.

Mine: a tunnel dug under castle walls by those laying siege to it.

Mangonel: a siege machine designed to attack castle walls.

Merlon: the stone part of the battlements at the top of a castle wall. See **crenel** and **embrasure.**

Meurtrière: French for murder hole. An opening in the wall of a gatehouse or barbican through which pikes could be thrust at attackers.

Motte: a mound. At first a natural or artificial hill on which castles were built.

Oubliette: a dungeon where prisoners were forgotten and left to starve to death.

Palisade: a line of stakes making a wooden defence. Used around the early baileys.

Portcullis: a heavy wooden or iron gate which could be raised or lowered. It was used principally for closing entrances or isolating attackers.

Postern: the rear gate of a castle (knights rode out of the gate, often unseen, to attack besiegers of the castle).

Siege: to attack a castle so as to prevent anyone leaving it.

Slight: to damage a building or tower so as to make it unusable.

Solar: a private room in a castle, usually in a sunny place.

Trebucket: a type of catapult used as a siege weapon.

THINGS TO DO

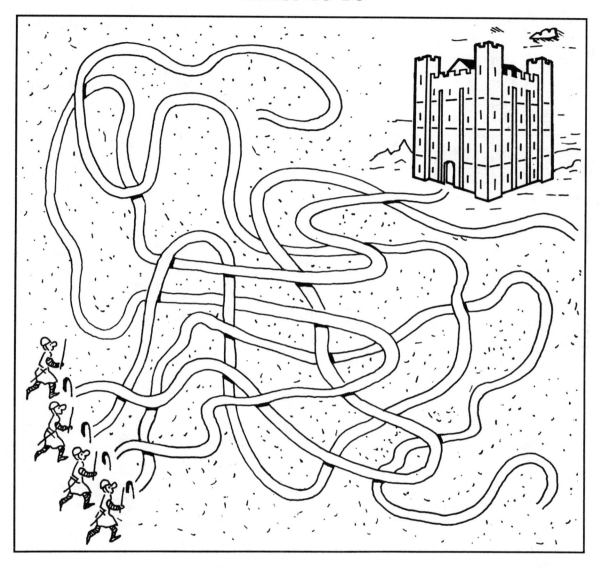

Which of these knights has found the secret passage under the castle?

1. Write an account of a visit to a castle.

2. If you were asked to build a castle, where would you build it? Draw a plan of your castle.

3. Imagine you are a squire. Write an account of how Baron Gilbert attacked the castle.

4. Imagine you are Lady Ann. Write an account of how the siege ended.

5. Do you think castles should be preserved? Which castle have you visited which has been well preserved?

6. What can you learn by visiting a castle?

ANSWERS

PAGE 11
2. Motte, keep, bailey, curtain wall, gatehouse, barbican, murder holes, portcullis, loop, moat.

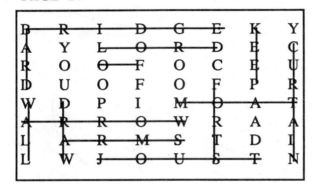

PAGE 14

PAGE 21
1. Arrows, catapult, siege engine, belfry, battering ram, sapping, mantlet, trebuchet, ladder, ballista.

2. c and e.
3. Knight.
4. Egg, gin, genie, is, seen, sign, sin, sine, sing, singe.

PAGE 24.
WE ARE BESIEGED.
      PLEASE SEND HELP.

R DROO HVMW URUGB
PMRTSGH ZG LMXV.

PAGE 27
1. Pendennis 2. Powderham
3. Berry Pomeroy
4. St. Michael's Mount
5. Castle Drogo 6. Tiverton
7. Sherborne 8. Dunster

PAGE 9

PAGE 29
CASTLES OF THE WEST COUNTRY

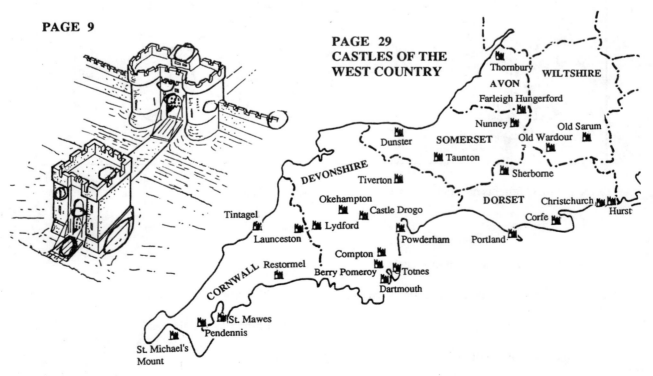

32